DIFFERENT
BUT
THE SAME

BY: Keyonna A Monroe

Illustrations by: Danh Tran

3G Publishing, Inc.
Loganville, Ga 30052
www.3gpublishinginc.com
Phone: 1-888-442-9637

First published by 3G Publishing, Inc., May, 2017

ISBN: 9781941247389

Printed in the United States of America

Hello reader let me introduce myself, my name is Paige and here's my dog scruff

WE JUST MOVED TO A NEW TOWN ON DIVERSITY LANE,
WHERE EVERYONE IS DIFFERENT, BUT ALL STILL THE SAME

Meet some of my friends, this is Jen and this is Lee

This is Micah and Ulla, and my bestest friend Kree

We each have a pet we're responsible for

Some that swim, some that walk, some that crawl on the floor

They eat different food and have different names,

EACH SHARE A HOME AND IS LOVED JUST THE SAME

My friend Lee is from China and Jen's from Brazil.
Each adopted by parents that live down the hill.

Lee goes hiking each week with his new mom and dad.

JEN'S NEW FAMILY GOES SAILING, AND SHE THINKS THAT'S RAD.

MICAH HAS A BIG FAMILY AND ULLA DOES TOO

Kree is from Ireland and has freckles like mine.
We love ice cream and pizza, so we get along fine

WE ALL RIDE OUR BIKES TO SCHOOL EVERY DAY

22

And after our lessons, we eat lunch and we play.

ON WEEKENDS WE GO TO THE NEIGHBORHOOD PARK,

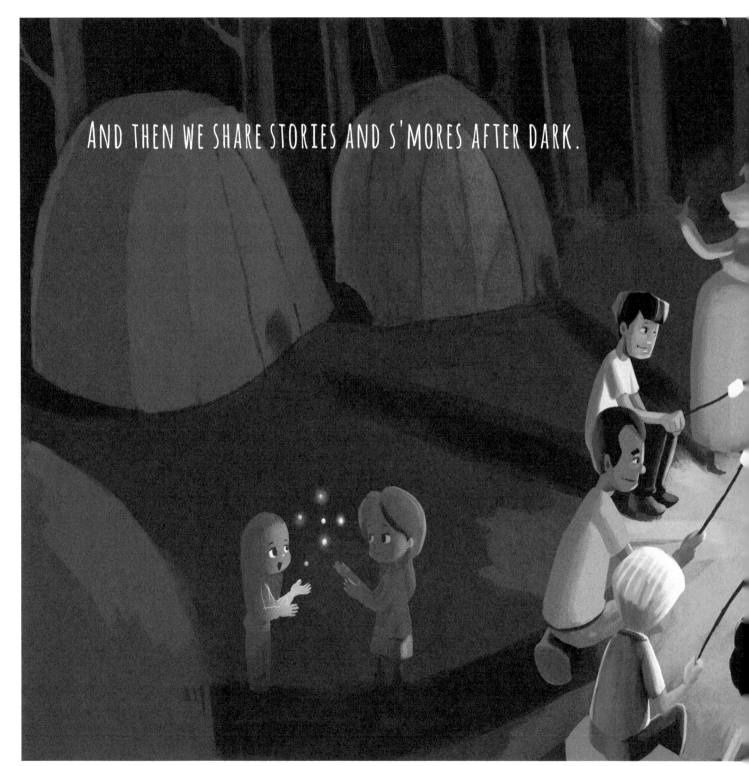

And then we share stories and s'mores after dark.

When we all go to bed, we're kissed, tucked in tight,
And safely assured that the bed bugs won't bite.

30

Oh, how I love this new town on Diversity Lane,
Where everyone's different, but we're also the same.

Kree is Irish and Swedish

Micah and his family
are Jamaican.

Ulla is biracial
Mom is Cuban, dad is Caucasian &
African American

...S FROM CHINA AND HIS
...LY IS FROM THAILAND.

JEN IS INDIAN FROM BRAZIL.

PAIGE'S MOM IS IRISH
AND DAD IS GREEK.

CPSIA information can be obtained
at www.ICGtesting.com
Printed in the USA
LVOW06s0502170817
545337LV00008B/23/P

9 781941 247389